BlAcK cIrcLes

LiFe

Katlyn Lipomi

ISBN: 151167413X
ISBN 13: 9781511674133

ACKNOWLEDGMENTS

To Mark C., my forever friend.

I hope I stay a kid at heart forever, always curious about everything. But as you grow up, you become wiser by hanging out with older people, because they explain and point out things about your own life that you thought you were still too young to experience and understand.

~Katlyn Lipomi

I've become a master
at breaking my own heart
with simple thoughts, dreams, and hopes
that are impossible to achieve.
Things that I will never accomplish,
places I will never go, and people I will never
be able to love
because my mind holds me back so very much.
It makes me sad and frustrated.
S.M. (2:09 a.m.)

1: *ELIZABETH*

You can be my cure, I will be your disease. You will end up saving me, but I will end up killing you.

My name is Elizabeth Headstrom.

At least, that's the other side of me.

My age does not matter. Neither does where I am from.

I view the world differently. Some would say I might have a mental disorder. It has not yet been diagnosed. No one ever took the time to find out.

I do, however, have a few things to say about life.

Some of the things I speak about I have experienced. Some I've learned through listening to people vent about their pathetic lives, and others I've witnessed.

Some can relate, others might get a reality check, and some might even disagree with me.

I've been taught to pick my battles so they are big enough to matter but small enough to win.

This is my battle. My battle with life.

Have you ever been beat down so many times you've stopped counting?

It's happened so many times you've lost all emotion.

You're just empty. Numb.

You're detached from yourself.

You can't stop sleeping and don't have any energy to even get out of bed to eat or shower.

You start having bizarre thoughts and strange dreams.

After a while your mind and soul have given up

by not having any emotions or feelings left.

Honestly, you just drive yourself to insanity when you have emotions.

But I like it.

It's war with myself that intrigues me—how your own mind can win over your life.

I've learned to accept it.

It prevents all the arguments and frustrations with people who do not understand.

I do miss myself when my memory asks how I'm doing.

I'm chasing a dream that's way out of my league.

I'm on a mission, but I don't know where I'm going.

I always felt out of place my whole life.

I was always told I was the black sheep.

I never really belonged anywhere.

I've been miserable with every single decision I've made.

Even if I faked a temporary act, I only did it to feel happiness.

Nothing has ever turned out OK.

Everyone was always in this box, and there I was on the outside looking in.

Everyone says I have this beautiful side, and then there's this side I try to hide.

I always seem to forget this side of me

that comes out and reminds me how unfriendly, lost, and lonely

I am on the inside.

This dark, deep side to me I have no control over.

I don't go any other way.

It's either the bright side or the dark side of me.

There isn't gray for me; it's either black or white or nothing at all.

They say I'm a child at heart but have an old soul.

I might have lived in a normal atmosphere,

but my life was anything but ordinary.

My whole life I've always felt like I am in a foreign country,

like I was shipped here from Mars.

Any outsider that drives by our house

might think, "What a nice family.

I wish I could have that. They have a nice house in a nice neighborhood

with nice jobs, and the kids go to a nice school."

Being naive to stereotypes is a very powerful assumption.

Almost like denial and oblivion,

which everyone encounters at least once in their life.

No one in my life has ever helped, either.

They were dysfunctional in some way. Not one was ever "normal."

I have something lost souls need.

I've taught myself how to say good-bye.

Broken people are drawn to me.

I give them what they need.

Then they set themselves free.

They say good-bye in different ways.

I have always felt like I'm being watched or under attack

everywhere I go.

I could be the first one in the room, just sitting there

minding my own business,

and somehow it never fails

I'm always the center of attention.

I take being paranoid to a whole different level.

I have to hide everything I do

because at some point

it will be used against me.

But yet they say there is nothing wrong with me,

so what is it?

Because I look in the mirror

and try to see what they apparently see.

I say there's nothing wrong with me,

but everyone can find a hundred things wrong with me.

I get anxiety about everything.

That is why I hoard my feelings,

just like how I hoard everything,

because the meaningless things I have

only mean something to me.

I become obsessed

with unimportant things

that go over and over in my head until

it eats away at me and makes me feel like I'm in a coma.

Maybe they leave because they're like mirrors: they see how I think of myself.

I'm banged up and exhausted from being a mess

mentally and physically.

But I leave a smile on my face

and a spark in my eyes

because that's just who I am,

the best actress alive.

Because being human is the most difficult thing to be.

I've learned to enjoy myself because I'm always alone

until the next one I meet falls in and out of my life.

They implant an image of you from when you were a child. They kept how you looked, how you smelled, and the way they felt when they looked at you. Time goes by, and every time they look at you, they still have that expectation that you should look like you did the last time they saw you.

~Katlyn Lipomi

2: *FAMILY*

Life becomes easier when you learn to accept an apology you never got.

~Robert Brault

I'm in denial about the people I'm supposed to love.

I'm sure they know deep inside they feel the same about me.

They act like they hate me.

I can tell just by the way they look at me in disgust that I'm disappointing them again.

It's weird to think that your parents have feelings, too, that they have deep emotions that they never speak about.

They might actually have the same story to tell, or close to it.

I mean, we are made by them, right?

The common thing we share is that our relationship is based on emotions that we ourselves can't understand.

It's like they want me around to feel loved by someone they made, but my imperfections don't meet their standards. Their way of thinking is that if it doesn't meet their standards, they will destroy it because that is what they were taught in life. This is how they handle things because this is all they know.

They always tell me I'm screwed up, but they refuse to look in the mirror themself, even though we all know the apple doesn't fall far from the tree.

I want them to see me as independent, but no matter what I do, I know they will never see me that way because they still wait for me to ask for help.

I feel like they never gave me enough credit for the person I can be.

I left because we tested and pushed each other over the edge.

They still become upset.

I know they love me. I know they will always be there for me.

They just do not know how to deal with elizabeth.

Then one day hell froze over, and they cried

when I told them I was sorry

because I'm not who they wanted me to be.

So I packed my suitcase and left my whole life behind

without a job or anywhere to live, just hoping to run away from whatever was consuming me.

I left without my heart, but I left it with them since I couldn't give them anything else.

It had tears and scrapes and was a little bruised and blemished, but I know they will cherish it because it's the only thing left that was a part of who I used to be.

I didn't have any use for it because I forgot how to love even myself.

They could no longer hold my hand, because it was time for me to move on.

I find it odd not a word was said as I walked out the door. We just stood there staring at each other with tears in our eyes.

They cried because they knew they had lost me.

I was crying because of the disappointments I'd given them.

I've learned you can't run away from yourself

or from the issues you're having.

You can't do it by moving place to place because you don't have a choice but to take yourself with you.

Not all of it is shattered. You can put the important things back together again.

You always think your parents will be there forever, but they have to let you go so you can fend for yourself.

Life's funny sometimes.

Just because your parents watched you grow

we realize that you've become just another person in the world.

Everyone comes into your life for a reason.
Even if they just passed by you or gave you a glance.
You thought something.
It showed more about your character.
When I first saw him, I looked at him like a book.
I judged the cover before I read the inside.
I found him physically unattractive.
I don't remember his name, but he changed my life after he said something that stuck with me, after only speaking to him for an hour or so.
I would consider him a friend because he told me you don't need to be a genius to be where you want to be in life.
You just have to find something you really enjoy doing.
Do it every day until you become an expert at it.
If you really have a passion for it, you won't forget to make it come true.
If it's meant to happen, everything will fall into place when it's supposed to.
He ended up showing me there is more to life than what I was going through at that time.
Sometimes people turn out to be beautiful when they say something from their heart.

~Katlyn Lipomi

3: *FRIENDS*

I've learned that people will forget what you said, people will forget what you did, but people will never forget how you made them *feel*.

Maya Angelou

They say it only takes one person to change your life, which is you. That's true, but it takes one person to point out the issue to you.

Everyone has had that friend who made them feel like someone.
They're either there to teach you something or show you something or you need something from them.
It happens very rarely, but there's always that one who stays with you forever.

They're like a miracle that points something out that your oblivious, delusional side needs to hear.

It's hard to find someone who is truly there for you, who wants you to succeed.
Everyone is two-faced. If they say they're not, they're liars as well.
They say all you need is that one friend, because not everyone will care enough about you.

I had a friend who meant more to me than anyone in my life.
It felt like our souls knew each other before our bodies met. I knew it from the moment I met her. It wasn't a romance or anything like that. I just knew there was something different about her. Sometimes you meet

someone, and it's obvious that you two are on the same level and belong to each other. You just know they will bring something to the table for you, and you become curious to know what it is. We weren't related. We were not lovers. We barely knew each other at first. We just clicked. No one understood it, not even us. You can't explain how you just fall in love with the feeling they bring to you. It felt like I'd known her my entire life. I've never met anyone like her before. They just have the power to make you feel like you're someone. I'm not sure if that made me believe in coincidence, destiny, or even fate, but there was definitely something there.

I was in denial about both of us being hurt. We were a peaceful war. We were at peace with each other but at war with ourselves and the world of trying to figure everything out but not having to grow up. We were both rebellious and were always getting into trouble. It started out as small things like skipping class or detention or even talking back to the teachers. We started getting in trouble outside of school. At first we never got caught, so in our heads there wasn't anything wrong with what we were doing. As time passed, the law started to get involved. People couldn't stand us after a while. They cringed when they saw us together. They were worried for us. But we were so blind. Maybe that's why I felt so connected to her. We had the same mind-set. We couldn't help ourselves.

We just could never bring ourselves to walk away from each other.

I was in denial about both of us being damaged souls. But at least she cared. No one else had.

The overpowering silence and the dirty glares when we would walk into the room together would cause so much tension. Built up like a gun waiting to go off on the elephants in the room.

I told her, "You scare me."

She asked, "Why?"

I answered, "It scares me that we met each other. You make me so happy, but lately you've been making me

sad and happy."
I told her, "I tell you things I can't even explain to myself." Even though I never got a straight answer, I still felt like I learned something around her.
What I wanted to say but never had was,
"You're making me sad because I know I'm losing you."
When she showed me she couldn't love herself anymore and she had forgotten that I loved her, it was then that it occurred to me that we were both dangerous.
It brought me to tears and made my heart sink into my throat
how she could make me so happy all day, every day, and now she could make me feel both happy and sad.
I hung on to the happiness as long as I could, even though I knew it wasn't really there anymore, because she had the power to take that away too when she disappeared.
But at least she still cared; no one else had.
People would look at us like we were a weird bug.
We didn't care. We had a bond like no one else had.
That no one could understand.
We were addicted to each other in a twisted way.
I promised myself I would never get hurt again, but I ended up loving her for the person she was and how I felt around her. It was 4:00 a.m., and we were talking about nothing that seemed so important to the both of us. We sat on the porch and laughed so hard without even saying a word.
I walked away feeling like I had just won the lottery.
I felt good about myself for the first time in a long time, and I knew I was screwed because she had won me over.
They say the emotion that can break your heart is sometimes the very one that heals it.
We have been through hell and back with each other.
It's definitely made me a part of who I am today.
I usually never tell people about my feelings, because then they learn something about me and end up defeating me. I always pushed them away.
I can say I never thought of pushing her away, and she never once tried to defeat me.

I know why we drifted apart.
I don't speak about it.
I remember it like it was yesterday, though.
I remember everything from that day because it changed my life forever.
It was October 2, 2009, roughly after 1:00 p.m.
It was sixty-eight degrees and partly cloudy with a little breeze.
We had stopped at this coffee place that was near my house.
I drove my gray Monte Carlo there.
As we waited in the car right in front of the place, we made a call to get some stuff.
After she had hung up, she made me back out of the spot and told me to make a right.
I don't remember the directions, but I do remember what the house looked like.
We waited for him to come outside. When we saw him peek his head out the door, we proceeded inside.
What happened in that house will forever be a hit of reality in the face for me.
I remember what the dispatcher's voice sounded like.
I remember what the paramedics looked like.
I remember watching her on the floor for a split second before two police stepped in front of me, blocking my view, and pulled me away from the scene.
I thought that was the last time I would ever see her again.
I sat on the patio chair they used as furniture in the house.
I could hear one of them shouting, "Hey, come back, can you hear me? Do you know where you are?" from downstairs.
They searched me, trying to find anything.
They didn't. I was escorted out.
When I turned around and saw her walking down the stairs with a mask on,
I had never had every emotion run through me at the same time before.

I went to say something, and they pushed me out the door more and told me not to talk.
I had so many questions to ask her, but I never got the chance to.
Years have gone by, and I've heard it only became worse.
The one thing that bothered me the most was that she had given up.
Her mother found her in the bathtub dead.
She survived, thank God.
I heard she had to get help a few times.
And it worked.
I also was told she got a tattoo on her ankle that reads "Serenity,"
with "October 2, 2009," underneath.
I will wait for her not only for her to love herself again, but for clarity.
Even though she never said good-bye, I know deep inside she already had, and I know she will say it one day to me in person.
What made us drift apart never tore us apart.
Her soul stayed with me, even though time has gone by and it's been years since we have spoken.
Her love will forever be imprinted in my heart.
We parted only in our bodies but never in our souls or our hearts.

4: _WORDS_

Sticks and stones may break your bones, but words can break your soul.

~Katlyn Lipomi

Bruises.
They're not always visible.
Words can beat you down just as easily as being physically beaten.
Words can destroy your soul and make you look at the world differently.
Maybe if we all were blind and deaf there would be peace.
Sticks and stones may break my bones, but words can never hurt me.
That's a false quote.
The truth of the matter is they can.
Words can eat your soul away.
It's a four-letter word that impacts every aspect of your life.
Words traumatized me.
My whole life I was told I was stupid and fat and would never amount to anything.
When you hear it from more than one person, you begin to believe it.
It prevented me from doing a lot of things I was capable of accomplishing.
They never gave me a chance because of my childlike behavior.
It ate away at me so much for years that I started to look at life negatively.
It changed where I was in life.

If it weren't for words, I'm sure I would have made better choices in my life and gone down a better path and be where I want to be now.

It's why I lived a lie to make my life seem better than it actually was.

I saw a black-and-white silent image that I imagined in my head.

I visualized what was going on around me but pretended I couldn't hear them talking to me.

With words you express more of how you feel about someone, because it's straight to the point, where when you get punched in the face, it takes longer to process that that person does not really care about you.

You don't say things out of anger. You meant what you said.

It was built up inside you for so long that when you were angry at me it finally came out, even if it had nothing to do with why you were upset at that moment.

It's just an excuse to finally say it.

You use "I said it out of anger" as an excuse to cover up a secret.

Everything changes and will never be the same after all is said and done. You sit and say everyone is to blame for the sorrow you drown in.

He always called me weird and said I was acting stupid because I loved dancing in the rain, eating dinner on the floor, wearing T-shirts and walking barefoot around the house, talking about anything at 3:00 a.m., learning new things, laughing for no reason at all, bursting into song and dancing to it, and making people laugh. He disliked my childish, spontaneous behavior. It was immature to him, and he never failed to let me know that. He instilled in my head that that's not how "normal" people act. He pointed out what I was doing wrong and called me names for misunderstanding something. I became the things he said.

I just shut down and turned into a robot when he was around.

I always thought he was right, that there was something wrong with me. It wasn't very long before I realized this is not the way to live. It was he who wasn't experiencing life, because he cared what people thought about him. You don't live by being boring and thinking you have to act a certain way. I can say I'm satisfied I never gave him the power to take that away from me. My character. My dignity. I became tired of replacing it with people who always tried to rob it. Maybe if we were all blind we wouldn't have the power to judge, so there wouldn't be anything to say.

Lust plus jealousy equals love⋯

I didn't love any of them. I just didn't want to feel
abandoned. I just wanted to know what love felt like. So
I stayed with them but wondered why I had to pretend
to feel it every day. Love makes you feel obligated to
reciprocate, especially when you do it in the moment. I
never loved them, because you don't damage and hurt
people you love.

~Katlyn Lipomi

5: *LOVE*

Never become too attached to anyone, because attachments lead to expectation and expectations lead to disappointments. ~unknown

If we deny love that is given to us, if we refuse to give love because we fear pain and loss, then our lives will be empty, our loss greater.

~Oprah Winfrey

I wish I was a different species.
I wouldn't have to deal with guilt, anger, greed,
envy, pain, hurt, and every other
emotion
we have!
Without it we wouldn't have
lost souls, drug addicts, mental facilities,
hookers, suicides, or abusive relationships
trying to find love.
We wouldn't have shattered dreams and hopes.
So why do we crave it?
Why are humans the only ones who need it?
Maybe we have too much freedom and we waste
it
on our favorite mistakes.
Satan created love
so we can lose our minds
and he can take over.

But then we question,
is there even a devil?
Who even knows if he really exists.
Why doesn't any other species know about him?
I'm not sure what's worse: being in love, being
lonely, or jumping off a bridge to drown.

MARRIAGE

There wouldn't be marriage to only
have to be tied down
to that one person the rest of your life.
Because love is sacred to those who have never
been married.
You wouldn't have regrets
of putting your dreams on hold
that you forget as days turn into years
and your routine
that has manipulated you
for all these years
is still going on.
You wouldn't have to put
your dreams and desires
on hold
to make that other person
happy and not leave you.
Love is the devil.
It has so many sides

of disappointment but also brings clarity and
happiness.
Love is every feeling and emotion
we feel.
Without it,
we wouldn't feel guilty
for not doing what really makes us happy.
We wouldn't be brainwashed into
thinking nothing is wrong
with this concept.
People, no matter how much
someone loves you,
never underestimate
their tendency to
not give a shit,
because they will act
contrary to their own interests
and leave you
in the cold to
fend for yourself.
People have told me I'm not mature enough to
have a relationship.
I respond with,
'I just haven't found anyone that doesn't
want me to be a robot
due to the fact they can't handle my madness,
my weirdness.'
Love doesn't mean anything anyway, because
unfortunately money is

more *integral*
to happiness than
romantic love.

SEX

Sex is overrated.
It's only a good thing
when you're not getting any
because all sex has consequences.
It will torture your emotions and thought
process.
Being with someone is like a
minor tragedy
because
no matter what,
you end up getting hurt
whether you're in denial or not.
Most people do it
because they're lost, hurt, and lonely.
That's why we should skip the bullshit
and act like savages
like we're supposed to anyway.
I don't understand
this whole lust and infatuation thing.
Why do we have different types
of love?
When you love someone, you care about them
and have every feeling

toward them.
You either love someone
or you don't.
Enough with
these other definitions of 'love.'
Lust is being used below the belt.
Lust is lewd. You look for that certain feeling
of being wanted by and attracted to someone.
It's sometimes a feeling you never received,
but you still wait for it like you have an idea
what it feels like.
It's being used to fulfill their needs.
It's nothing more than sexual tension.
Having attraction to someone doesn't mean you
love them.
You might have thought you loved them,
only to find out you were only attracted to them
before you became bored with them.
Love is a control thing
while attraction and lust are a minor free-for-
all.
Love turns you twelve years old again.
They turn into your parents,
always asking who you're going out with, what
time you will be home.
You have to involve them in everything you do.
Love is different from attraction.
Love can ruin your life.

Lust can only ruin some things you
subconsciously needed to let go of anyway.
Love is an unexplained
feeling
that we will never
understand.
It's the same feeling as being lonely.
As much as love is a horrible emotion,
sometimes
it might shed light in the dark areas of your life.
Then I met him.
It turned out to be an obsession.
More than the word 'infatuation,' to say the least.
I had something he fell for.
Then he caught me.
He found out why I kept trying to run away from
him.
To this day I will never have clarity.
I will always wonder every single day about
what went wrong that first day in May.
It goes through my head
every moment of the day.
It was impossible to understand
what was going through his head
when he never understood it himself.
Maybe all it took
was my lost smile
to injure his soul,
and I will never know how

broken he really was.
For he was attracted to my angels
but fell for my demons.
That last phone call
for him to say
his last good-bye
will be the first thought in my head every day
for the rest of my life.
But even though
I don't know how to love,
I had an idea.
I knew the definition.
I knew the signs.
Maybe I just didn't want to lose
my ability to think rationally because of my affection.
I just didn't know or want to do it.
Unfortunately, I couldn't
bring myself to do it.
He knew how.
He tried to teach me.
But he
couldn't get past the demons
to teach my angels who were willing to learn.
I shouldn't have let him
get involved with me.
I told him, 'Sorry, you're not the first
person I think of
when I first open my eyes to the sunlight,'
but I loved that
he was drawn to me.
You're so consumed with making them happy,
with their pleasures and needs,
you forget yours.

It doesn't make sense to let go
of something you had for so long, but it also
doesn't
make sense to hold on when there's nothing
there.
I destroyed him in a beautiful way.
He was angry at me,
had so much hate toward me
for destroying
not only him
but his whole life.
He has every right to hate me.
But why should he?
Because of me he will finally see how unpleasing
his life really was.
I think I just took him by surprise
with what I had to show him.
They say love is free.
That's not true, because the plane ticket
he bought to say good-bye was $400.
I loved his attention, his affection. I just didn't
know how to love him.
He told me, "You can't love someone until you
can love yourself."

I asked,
"Why do we have to love anyone?"

6: *HAPPINESS*

The happiest-looking people are the most broken inside.

~Katlyn Lipomi

Happiness.

I'm not sure what that word really means.

It's been a while, and even then I don't think I really understood it. I was naive and hadn't experienced life yet.

The last time I recall being happy was when I was looking upside down at the back of my house.

My arms dangling and my legs becoming numb from hanging off the monkey bar, being spaced out with nothing going on in my head. Or the time I would dress up in different costumes and pretend to be someone or something else, or lying in the grass looking at the sky trying to make something out of the clouds.

I had a few memories, but they're too far in the past that it's just a lost memory that when my memory misses it, he brings it up and reminds me of them every now and again.

It's scary what a smile hides. Fake happiness is the worst sadness, like a happy drunk who's not really a happy person.

Sometimes all it takes is that one person to show you the missing puzzle piece you were looking for, and ironically it's usually the one person you were least expecting anything from.

They tend to show you how you're missing the happiness you used to have, that you are in such denial about how you've been hiding it. It's ironic, isn't it, that when you forget what you were chasing, one person brings it back to you without even having a clue what they have just done. The one that just falls into your life.

It is amazing what you get from someone when you don't go looking for it. It might be subconscious and they hold a red flag, or maybe it's God saving you from a mistake you can't take back.

He lived near me. I never knew his name. I might have walked past him a few times, but I would have never acknowledged him. It was like he was waiting for that perfect moment to stumble into my life right before I was about to jump off a cliff. Everyone that comes into your life has an impact and is there for a reason. It's like you have something in common, but you barely even know each other's last names.

Angels are not invisible. They don't fly around and wear white. They don't fall out of the sky; they fall into your life. They're just normal people like you and me, waiting for that perfect moment to fall into your life and save you from yourself. They show you and protect you from something you always knew was there but never paid attention to, and that will some day at some point abandon you.

I would say angels are broken people missing something in their lives, and only you, for some reason, have the answer to the equation. I would call him an angel. I received something more than just a business plan we had discussed.

As unhappy as I was, I think I figured it out. I didn't need a pill to pretend I was happy. It wasn't fixing anything, just covering up my depression, fogging my eyes, and tricking my brain into thinking something had finally changed, that magically I was happy. It never fixed what was really making me unhappy. It's not a chemical imbalance or your emotions that need to be met; it's your environment.

Happiness is not about what kind of car you drive, how big your house is, what you do for a living, and how much you make. It's about waking up every morning not wanting to change anything and accepting who you are and how you look at the negative imperfections in your life. Being happy is being satisfied, and taking a pill to feel satisfied is not being happy when you have to hide certain things to make your life look better than it is.

Pain is like a current. It takes you places you never wanted to go, and since you're sucked in, it's too hard to get out without someone there to help save you because you can't do it alone.

I believe he is an angel. I received more than just happiness. I received love, a special kind of friendship, and a learning experience.

Even if I wanted to repay him, he would say, "It won't be necessary. You've already done so by returning the same favor."

I was missing my puzzle piece that he had for a very long time. He gave it to me at the perfect time before I lost my mind.

That's why destiny at some point might actually save you from yourself.

Everyone I've ever met has given me a box of darkness as a welcoming present. But I never understood what to make of it or what to do with it. After so many times of receiving the same gift from everyone, that I could never refund. I finally took the time to see what was inside, after he gave me the box. So I didn't have a choice but to accept it. He was telling me you have to appreciate pain to appreciate happiness.

Why him out of billions of people in the world? I will probably never know the answer to that, and I don't think I want to because I'm happy with the results.

We both stumbled into each other's lives to give each other the box and show how truly unhappy we really were deep inside. We were not looking for it. It just kind of happened.

It's funny how the only reason why some people stay here on earth is because their nine year old heart told them to follow their dream that will never happen. But deep down inside they still have so much hope and the expectation that it will.

~Katlyn Lipomi

7: *MONEY AND HOPE*

Many people are so poor because the only thing they have is money. ~unkown

Too many people buy things they don't need with money they don't have to impress people they don't know.

~*Rich Dad, Poor Dad*

Money doesn't show you anything but denial. It hides one's true self. It doesn't show you what you are missing in life. It will only show you a surreal world with fake friends, a fake husband or wife, even a fake child who will only stop complaining when you've given in.

It has the power to ruin your ego. While you think you're someone, everyone else is laughing at you. It can leave you with unclarity and brainwash you and leave you mindless. Most people will do anything for it. They would rather be miserable with money than not have it at all. It has the power to make you unhappy or make you think everything is OK. It can cover up who you really are or even change you into something you're not. Even if you have it, you will always find yourself thinking about what you're missing.

So we buy big, expensive, nice things to impress people we don't even like to prove we're better than them. It's an insecurity issue a lot of us seem to have.

It's obvious we do it because we're not happy with our lives, but in the end it means nothing to them.

Deep down you care so much about what people think about you. Sometimes it leads to a never-ending competition that no one ever wins. You don't realize this, but you should just give it up now because you've won already by making them believe you have it better than them. It's sad how money can make you act insane. Money will drive you crazy. It will make you fiend for it more than wanting love. They say a rich man once said, "Money isn't everything," because he forgot what it's like not to have any.

Money takes over your life. It takes up hours of it. Money has the power to destroy you, upset you. You need it to pay bills and feed yourself. Without it you can't do that. It can make you scam people, hurt people, empower people for it.

Money can make you look powerless. It can make yoou feel worthless. It can make have entitlement, or feel powerful. Money can easily be confused with love.

Money really is the root of all evil.

<u>Hope</u>.....

In reality, hope is the worst of all evils, because it prolongs the torments of man.

~Friedrich Nietzsche

Hope is hoping to make something of yourself without having to work for it. Hope is an idea you get in your head that everything will follow your thoughts and come true. The thing is, you're not a child anymore. None of that exists. You cannot pretend anymore. So why do we continue to do it? But sometimes when we do get it, it's not how we imagined it to turn out. We forget that nothing ever goes the way we envisioned it.

Hope is the denial of reality.

I have waited to be an adult since I was twelve. When I turned eighteen, only a few things had changed. I could do everything but buy alcohol or rent a car. I still wasn't an adult—maybe by law, but not to the wise or even really to myself.

It wasn't until I had a meltdown that I finally lost it. That I ran away not just from my life but to different states thinking it would all go away. And I still had the nerve to wonder why nothing was fixed. Nothing had changed. I was still lost. Everything was still there, just further away in distance, and the loneliness was still lingering.

They say age is just a number, which is a fact, because reality is learning. There is no such thing as being an adult when you're forty and still unhappy with your life and still not wise enough to understand how to fix what went wrong. And the only thing that has changed is you've just grown older.

~Katlyn Lipomi

YOU ARE NOT ANY BETTER AS THE CEO THAN THE PERSON
WHO IS MOPPING THE FLOORS.

8: *WORK/JOBS*

You are being called to live a bigger life. Answer the call. Playing small does not serve you.

~Les Brown

A job is just to pay the bills, where as a career is part of who you are.

~Katlyn Lipomi

I believe the good people are broke because money is the root of all evil. Your eyes are groggy from the five hours of sleep you got before now waking up again to go back to or on to your other job. You put on what you think are nice clothes that you bought for five dollars, still trying to hold on to any dignity you have left.

I know what a worthless check means. You slave putting all these hours in, and somehow you're still broke. And you hope to God you don't become ill or injured because there isn't another way to pay the bills for a while.

I get pleasure watching these lost souls working so hard for their useless paycheck. I feel wiser because I know I'm not stuck here forever. They stand there with their hopeful smiles pretending to be better than they are. They act like they enjoy coming to work and just love seeing you every day. They have to act like a moron just to be able to laugh so they don't feel like a slave. They try so hard for that raise they were promised, telling themselves it will solve everything. Most people do it because they don't have anything else in life other than their cigarettes and broken promises. They don't care about you. They just use you.

Anyone higher than you doesn't care about you; you're just another person in the mix of making money for them. All they do is judge you. You work all these hours and still have nothing to show for it. You barely can pay your bills. You think, "Maybe I should just be a criminal or be in the sex industry where they get paid tons of money and don't have to understand anything."

9: *DENIAL*

You cannot change what you refuse to confront.

Anonymous

Definition: de·ni·al

dəˈnīəl/

noun

A pattern of failures; a kind of practical atheism or chosen ignorance among many believers and clergy. Disbelief in the existence or reality of a thing.

Denial is a source of protection.
It's protecting something you never want shattered.
It's our defense mechanism so we don't feel pain.
It has the ability to lower you into submission without even touching you or knowing your name. It blinds you from seeing the truth so your mind can be at ease only because it's not reality. Denial takes up most of your brain.
Denial is like someone standing behind a board. You know they're there, but you avoid acknowledging the fact they're actually standing there.
You begin to believe denying that anything is wrong with how they act.
They say they care, but they wear their fake smiles around their faces.
They wait for you to fall flat on your face.
That's what they want so they can feel better about themselves.
When you become an adult, no one cares. No one will help you. Most won't even look at you.
I was in denial about myself for a very long time.

I hated everything going on in my life.

I felt trapped. I was better off being incarcerated. At least then I wouldn't be in denial about my pathetic life.

It hides your happiness.

It turns you into a fool to believe this fantasy.

It's something in our lives that we think we need, but we really just need to stop doing it and face reality.

It's sometimes an insecurity thing. You know you want something more; you just don't know how to change it because you have been in it for so long. You don't want to destroy your fantasy, or else you will feel lost.

It lingers inside our heads. We know it's wrong, but we can't seem to plot our way out of it.

Time will distance you. "It's not like the way it was when I first met her. She wore a smaller dress size, and her hair was always done. We would only laugh and never fight. She was my best friend, my everything. Time will distance you, allow you to become strangers and not allow you to be as happy anymore. Now we barely even look at each other. We just go through the motions of our daily routine. I haven't felt her skin since I can remember. It makes me wonder what is under other pretty young girls' skirts more than I ever had before. If it were up to me and the opportunity presented itself, I think I would do it without hesitation. Time is supposed to heal things, but as you get older, it just fades things away into nothing," the elderly man at the bar said.

10: *TIME*

The more real you get, the more unreal the world gets.
~John Lennon

Growing old is unavoidable, but never growing up is possible. I believe you can retain certain things from yur childhood if you protect them. Certain traits, certain places where you don't let the world go. ~Johnny Depp

It feels like just yesterday we would roam our neighborhoods. All we did was care for one another. No matter the day we were always bold. Never saw gray. Not a thing in the world to care or worry about other than having our hopes and dreams come true one day, or to wonder why we couldn't touch the sky or when the ice cream man would arrive.

We wondered what we would be when we were old. We were determined to fulfill everything we wanted to be, from a teacher to a doctor and even an astronaut. We were going to do it all before life was a struggle, when we still had our whole lives ahead of us. When we didn't have to struggle to be happy. Would we still walk down the same road or move away? Which ladder would we take? Would our curiosity and imagination fade away? Would we always have one another until our dying day? For our footprints will be forever engraved in our parents' driveways.

We had nothing to prove, were friends with everyone. We could pretend in our heads to be anyone or anything anywhere in the world. Passing the time away with our curious creativity about everything. Excited and impatient for the time to come when we were all grown up and would be who we said we would be. Believing so strongly in everything. Trying to catch Santa and the tooth fairy. We buckled up our hearts in the backseat to drive away with our dignity and pride, looking out the window trying to find our next journey.

We miss the days when our siblings were our best friends, when we did everything together before we drifted away. Now we just work and pay rent and go about our own lives. Back when we didn't want to come inside because our nights were too much fun, we didn't want to miss anything. When we would fall asleep anxious and worried we wouldn't make it in time to meet at the cardboard box at 8:00 a.m. We had fun doing nothing, turning nothing into something. When the days used to pass slowly. Before the days turn into months and months into years. Simple-minded and innocent, we were. Before we blinked and all that disappeared, and we were all grown up with responsibilities and real fears. Realizing that life used to be a fairy tale. When we used to hold on to let go, because now we try to freeze time by dreading becoming old. For they will laugh in your face if you try to pretend again because that is immaturity that we're not allowed to have anymore. Time passes your innocence away. But my childhood days will forever be a part of me, locked in my heart to never be set free.

Attention through Time

I enjoy the attention I get from men and women. It
makes me feel attractive. I hold on to it because I will
one day grow wrinkles and my hair will turn gray
instead of growing longer. I will not walk as straight
anymore. I won't get this attention anymore. My
husband will notice the newer-model girls, and he will
not have a glow in his eye when he sees me anymore.

Trying Not to Let Go

So please tell me why we still become upset over
things. It was never perfect in the first place; it was
going to break at some point. People say good-bye in
different ways. They will leave you after they smile in
your face. As time passes people grow apart. They get
what they need from you, and all that's left is flashes of
the memories of all of us every now and again. When
we think about one another, we remember everything
about why, at that time, certain people impacted our
lives and what their reasons were for entering our
lives. But it was time to move on with our lives, I guess.
What you receive from them is up to you.

Eye's View

Everything in this life is either black or white. There
isn't any gray. So we try to add color, and when it
finally shows every now and again, we still sit there
and wait for it to come. Like being used for so-called
love. It's the same excited feeling. Then when it's done,

you go your separate ways. You wonder why that feeling went away because it's life. Everything is dark and fake. It's what we discover as we grow older and discover more about life.

Why Are We Here?

They say you're here to fulfill tasks in your life. You do them before you die. What's our purpose in life? Does everyone have one? I believe we do, just that some people never see it. Maybe that's why we become old, because we are still waiting for our purpose. But what about a homeless man? It must be his simple purpose to be placed there for your help so maybe you can feel better about yourself. With nothing to give, nothing to offer, he was blind to see the reason he existed.

Reality

Reality continues to hurt my soul, because my life is like a circle. Time flies by, and every situation comes back around, just with different people. I talk in such circles that no one can understand me at times. They say I'm different, hard to handle. I'm under the assumption that's why they always leave.

What's Worse?

Time is more surreal than love. It does heal things but makes us hold on to certain things that we should let go of. No matter how old we become, we never actually find ourselves. We never fully understand who we are as people.

Life is all just memories.

I, Elizabeth Headstrom, have a tendency to lose myself sometimes. I see the glass as full because I'm scared to lose something that I feel is important, even when it's not, because my mind will eat away at me if I don't look at every angle of every situation. I know I'm not the only person in the world who views life in such a negative way. The truth is, life is negative. There's more negative than positive, and you have to struggle for any kind of happiness. I don't know where these feelings came from. They have been there as long as I can remember. I just never really paid that close attention to them because I became so used to dealing with my psychotic mind. Do yourself a favor: ignore your mind and pay attention to your heart.

Maybe we need everything to fall apart. Maybe we need to hit rock bottom so we can see we needed to get out and get away from what was consuming us···Dark times will help you see the light only if you're wise enough to see it and learn from it.

~Katlyn Lipomi

My life is like a circle. I go through the same things just with differnet people and different places in every situation. I talk in circles when I am upset, scared, nervous or excited. Some things just never change I guess.